Tracy Hitchcock

AN OPEN AND LOVING HEART

An Open and Loving Heart

Gentle Words of Self-Endearment

Suzanne Hirabayashi

Artwork by
Aurea van Hoorn

DeVorss Publications

ISBN: 0-87516-701-2
Library of Congress Catalog Card Number: 97-67053

First Edition, 1997

DeVorss & Company, Publisher
P.O. Box 550
Marina del Rey, CA 90294

Printed in Hong Kong

This book is dedicated to my son,
Jake.

◎

Special thanks to Mer-Mer Chen

AN OPEN AND LOVING HEART

*A*cceptance

Love is the greatest force we know. It is the glue that binds us together. It is the healer of all wounds. Only an open heart knows love.

To open your heart you must only be willing. From that point on you will move into the place of acceptance. This is where love grows.

An open heart accepts oneself genuinely, accepts change easily, and views others tenderly.

ℬalance

Balance of mind, body, and spirit is the key to living a joyful and productive life.

Balance requires the discipline to ''make time'' for the different activities that nurture your different needs.

When your time is balanced, you exhibit calm behavior, clear judgment, and harmonious relationships.

Bring balance into your life and experience the joy of successful living.

Compromise

Love is never selfish or unkind. It always makes room for another person's wishes.

Compromise is the ability to make decisions that allow *both* partners to feel respected and empowered by the relationship.

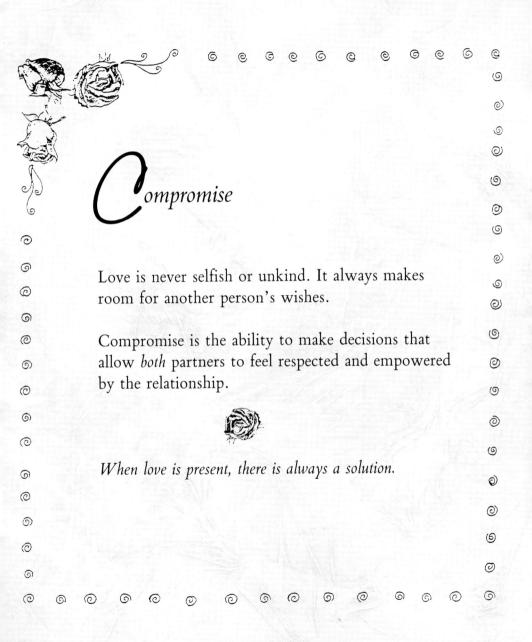

When love is present, there is always a solution.

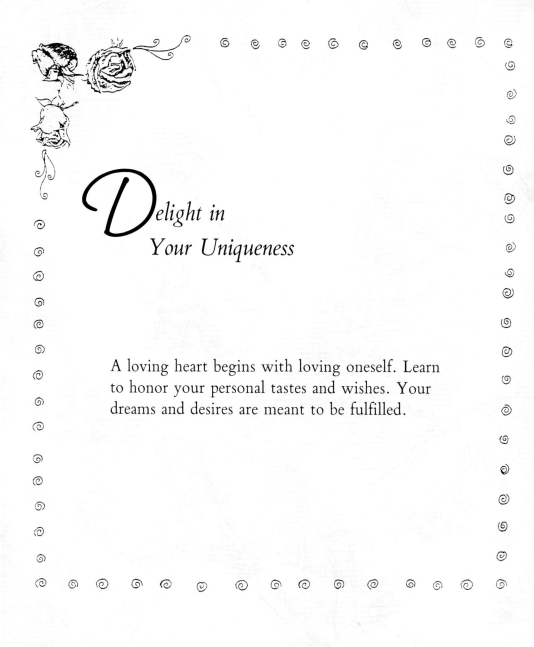

Delight in Your Uniqueness

A loving heart begins with loving oneself. Learn to honor your personal tastes and wishes. Your dreams and desires are meant to be fulfilled.

Dare to venture into the unknown with or without a partner. Depend on no person, place or thing for your happiness. Look within and you'll discover you have all that you need.

Love frees.

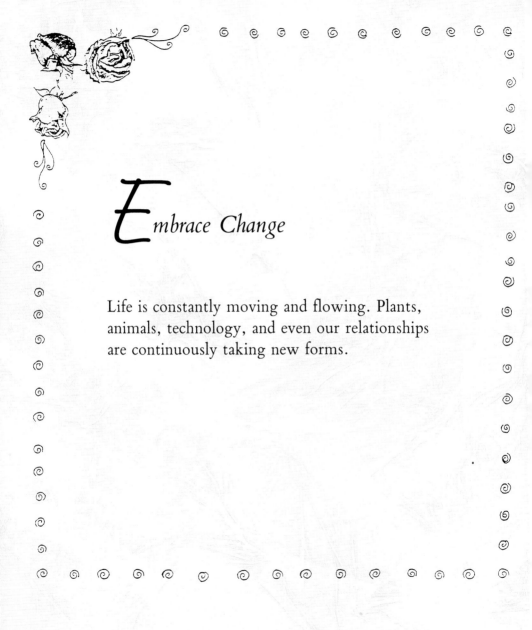

*E*mbrace Change

Life is constantly moving and flowing. Plants, animals, technology, and even our relationships are continuously taking new forms.

How we *feel* is based upon our perception of change. If you find yourself resisting change, be gentle with yourself. Shine some light on the situation and ask yourself: "What is it that I fear?" or "What do I think I'll lose?"

Let the answers be revealed. Make no judgments.

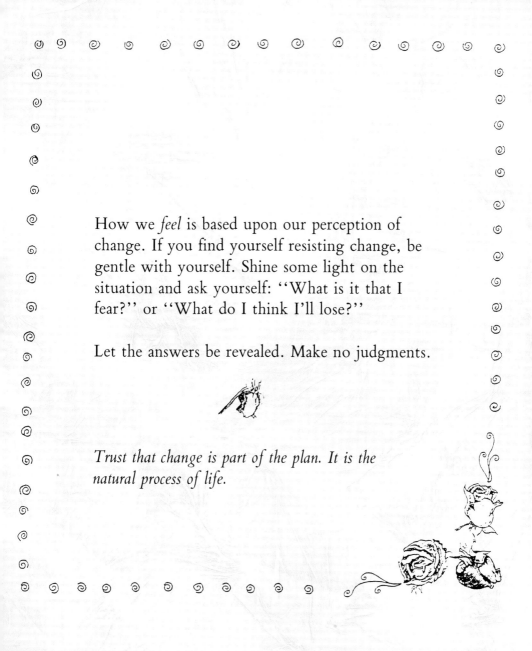

Trust that change is part of the plan. It is the natural process of life.

Forgiveness

The ability to forgive easily is truly an elixir to the mind, body, and soul.

Learn to forgive yourself and others for mistakes and transgressions.

Hanging on to grudges blocks our ability to function at our highest level and causes negative chemical reactions in the body.

Let go and love!

Focus on what is good and beautiful within yourself
and others.

Forgive easily and you will experience love's
abundant flow in all areas of your life.

Give of Yourself

Be free and joyful in your giving. Set no limits on the amount of love you can give. There is an endless supply of love in the universe and you can forever tap into it.

Love is meant to be shared with others. Give your time with a smile: it will be more greatly appreciated.

Give compliments freely; uplifting words heal the human spirit.

Give knowledge in a patient, gentle manner and learning will take place.

It costs nothing to give of your spirit, so give abundantly to all who cross your path.

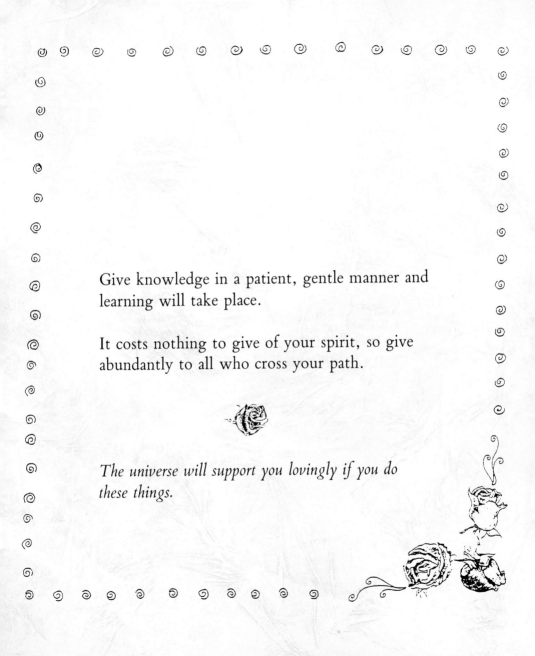

The universe will support you lovingly if you do these things.

$\mathcal{H}$ugs and Kisses

There are many types of hugs and kisses. Some are passionate; some are tender; and some are warm, friendly greetings.

No matter which kind, each is a wonderful way to exchange love without words.

Love heals. Open yourself up to opportunities to share affection with others.

Being able to give and receive affection easily is the sign of an open and loving heart.

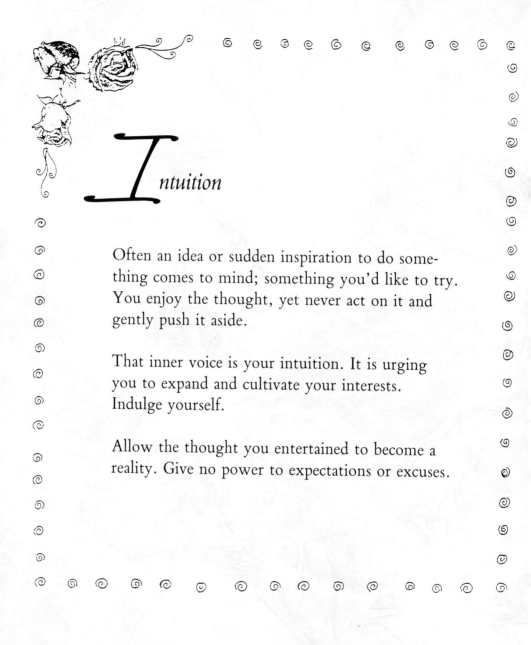

Intuition

Often an idea or sudden inspiration to do something comes to mind; something you'd like to try. You enjoy the thought, yet never act on it and gently push it aside.

That inner voice is your intuition. It is urging you to expand and cultivate your interests. Indulge yourself.

Allow the thought you entertained to become a reality. Give no power to expectations or excuses.

Your intuition will always lead you to the highest place of joy for your soul's growth. Where there is joy, there is love.

Joyful Spirit

A joyful spirit *welcomes* life and all of its surprises.

A joyful spirit is a warm heart that laughs often and knows that, despite the bleakest of outward conditions, all is well.

A joyful spirit can overcome any trial or tribulation, because where there is joy, there is love, and where there is love, there is healing.

A joyful spirit knows the truth.

$\mathcal{K}$eep Your Word

Relationships are successful when partners are able to trust and rely on each other's words.

Keeping your word is an honorable feat.

The ability to keep your word in small situations builds confidence and credibility in the relationship.

If you can exhibit integrity in the smaller circumstances of life, it is likely you'll do the same in more demanding situations.

Keep your word and you create a lasting bond.

*L*et Go

Know that you have the power to choose to live in the present moment. You deserve to be happy and free, so let it be!

You can let go of past hurts; you don't have to continually replay them in your mind or in your relationships. Use the past to understand, then let it go. Leave it behind.

Make new and better choices in the here and now.
Let go and live in the present moment.

*M*ake Time for the People in Your Life

Life is about relationships. Each person in your life is a gift. Treat them that way.

Make time to share your life with those you care about. Let there be joy and laughter in your relationships.

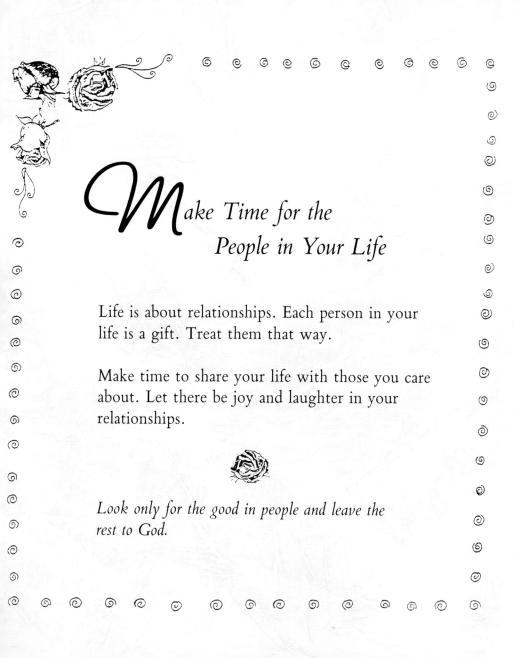

Look only for the good in people and leave the rest to God.

No Need to Judge

When you judge yourself or others, you limit expression. Judgment is similar to the clipping of a bird's wings. The bird still has the ability to fly, but it will never soar as high or as freely as it was meant to. Natural expression is limited.

When you let go of judgment and accept yourself as you are now, in this moment of time, love exists. You are free. Free to fly as high as you want.

Once love exists in you, you are able to see it in others.

We are all mirrors to one another, reflecting back to ourselves our own beliefs. So, whatever qualities you notice in another, be conscious that on some level those same qualities exist within you as well.

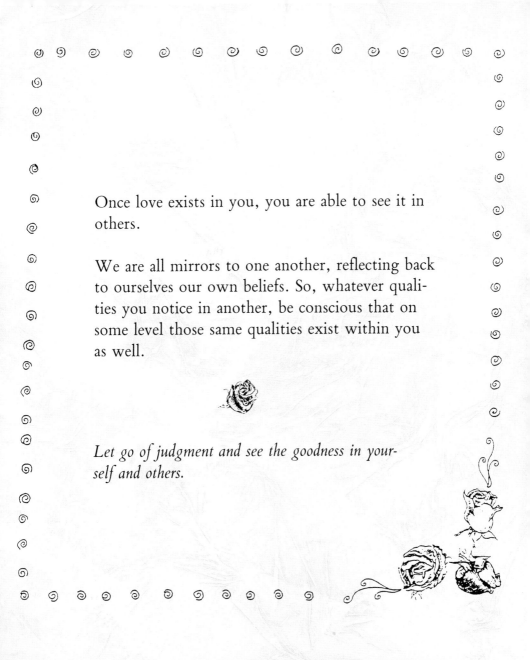

Let go of judgment and see the goodness in yourself and others.

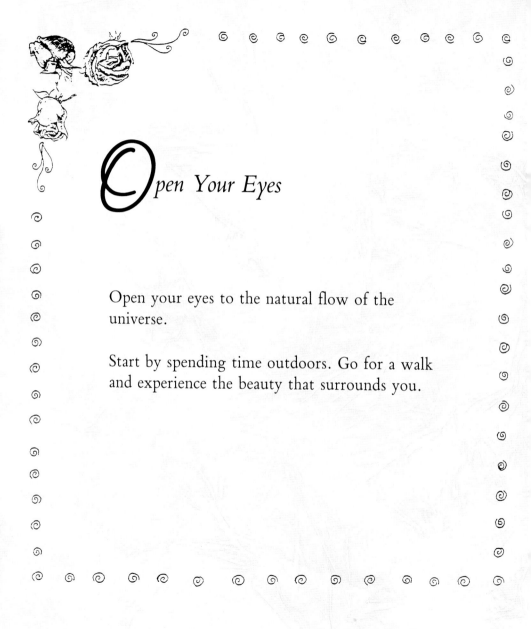

*O*pen Your Eyes

Open your eyes to the natural flow of the universe.

Start by spending time outdoors. Go for a walk and experience the beauty that surrounds you.

Look at the sky above; smell the trees and flowers as you pass them by; enjoy the sound of the birds chirping; feel the breeze on your skin; notice everything.

Open your eyes and know that there is much more to life than the bustle of your daily routine.

Open your eyes and feel the peace.

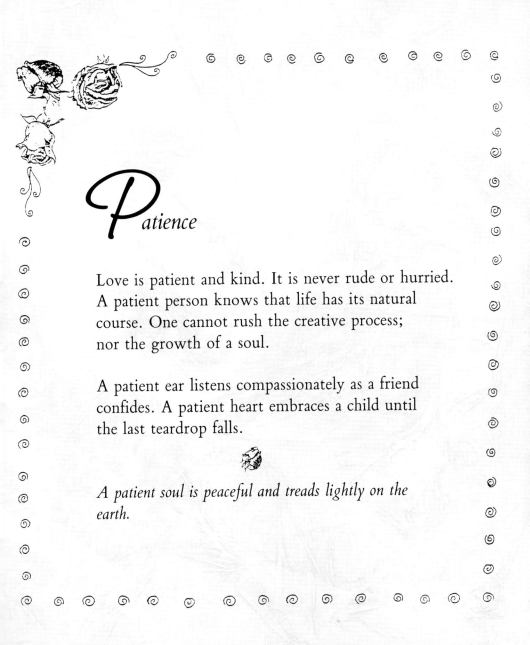

*P*atience

Love is patient and kind. It is never rude or hurried.
A patient person knows that life has its natural
course. One cannot rush the creative process;
nor the growth of a soul.

A patient ear listens compassionately as a friend
confides. A patient heart embraces a child until
the last teardrop falls.

*A patient soul is peaceful and treads lightly on the
earth.*

*Q*uiet Time

Quiet time is that precious space where spirit can speak to soul. It is a time of relaxation and rejuvenation.

Take time daily to close your eyes, tune in to your breathing, and let go of all cares.

Indulge yourself. Even if it is only for ten or fifteen minutes a day.

Allow yourself the privacy to experience the calm and peace of mind that quiet time gives.

Trust that this time empowers you.

Radiate Love

Radiate love and goodwill to others. Let the room become illuminated with your presence. Remember, attitudes are contagious. As you go higher, the whole room goes higher.

Oftentimes, we dim our light by holding back our feelings. We fear we'll appear foolish or we'll lose love. The truth is, we deny ourselves and others love when we limit our expression.

Let your light shine brightly and magnificently. Let light and love pour forth from all parts of your being.

$\mathcal{S}$implify and Direct Your Life

Life is like a garden; it needs organization, nurturing, occasional weeding, and watering in order to flourish.

A life with direction and planning is a life of purpose and fulfillment.

Nurture yourself along the way. It is a tender
gift you give yourself that will promote growth.

Weed out the draining people and chaotic activities
in your life. They suck up the creative life force.

Saturate your mind with positive, focused
thoughts of your goals.

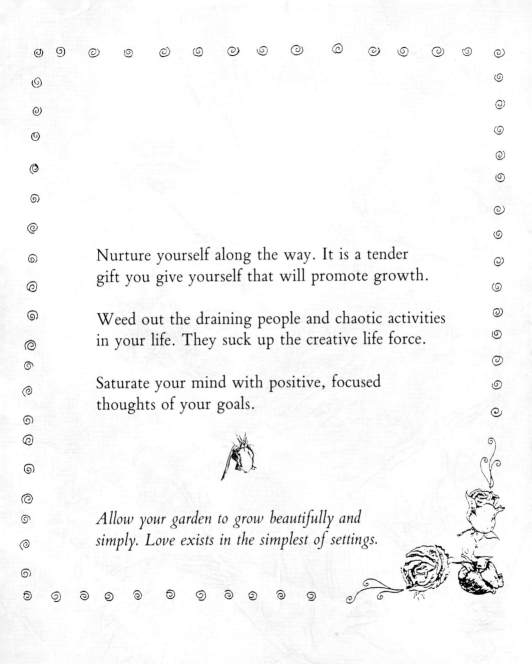

*Allow your garden to grow beautifully and
simply. Love exists in the simplest of settings.*

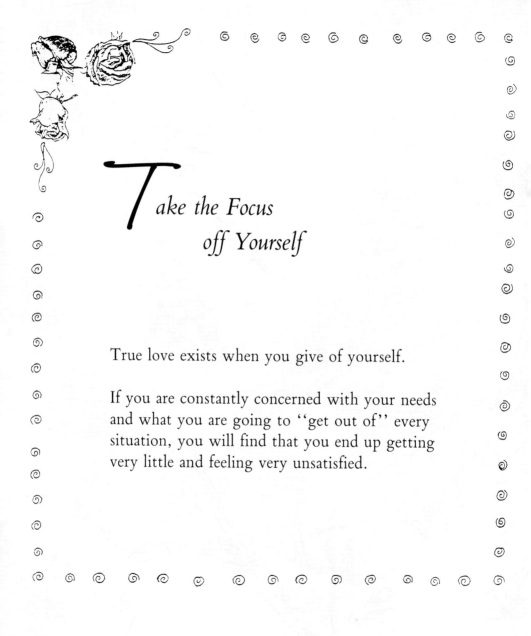

*T*ake the Focus
off Yourself

True love exists when you give of yourself.

If you are constantly concerned with your needs and what you are going to "get out of" every situation, you will find that you end up getting very little and feeling very unsatisfied.

One of the best ways to get out of a bad mood is to remove the focus from yourself and your situation and give love to someone else.

When you give, you'll discover a new energy coursing through your body.

You'll gain a renewed and refreshed outlook to face your challenges.

$\mathscr{U}$nderstanding

Understanding is the union of intellect and heart.
It is the ability to place yourself in others' shoes
in order to comprehend, feel, and experience
their viewpoint.

An understanding person doesn't judge, nor does
he feel the need to be "right."

Understanding is a realization of truth. It is a
personal commitment to an open and loving heart.

To understand is to love.

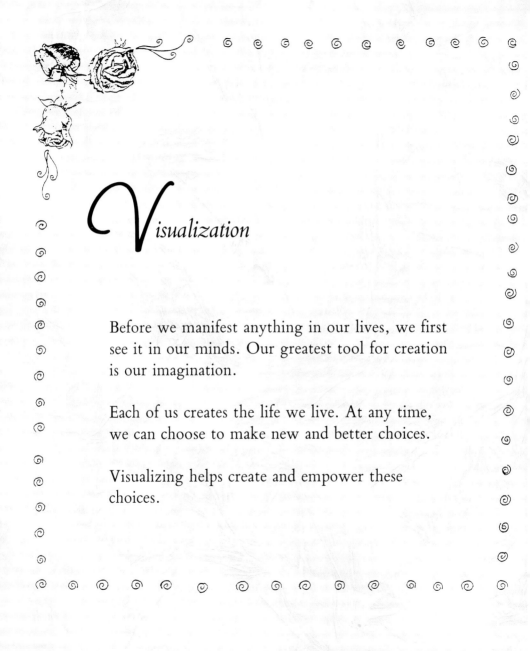

$\mathcal{V}$isualization

Before we manifest anything in our lives, we first see it in our minds. Our greatest tool for creation is our imagination.

Each of us creates the life we live. At any time, we can choose to make new and better choices.

Visualizing helps create and empower these choices.

Get specific about what it is you want: vibrant health, loving relationships, the perfect job, or whatever good desire you may have.

Visualize this choice daily. Allow the pictures to unfold in the most pleasing way your heart desires.

Set no limits!

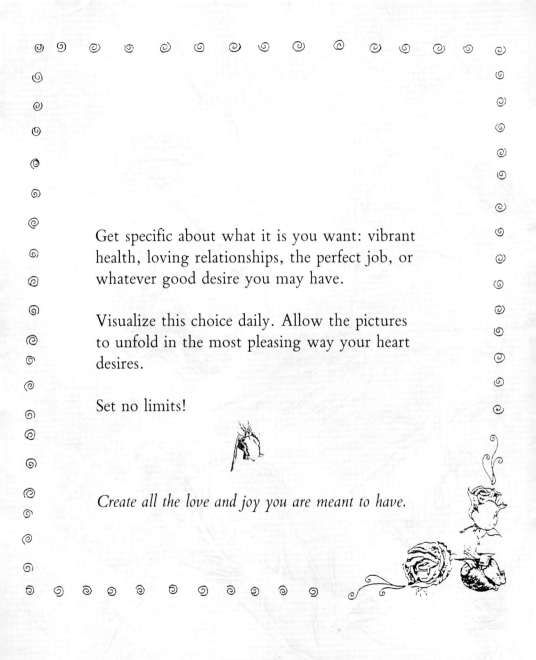

Create all the love and joy you are meant to have.

Walk Away from Anger

Walking away from an upset is really difficult to do, but it is a wonderful way to balance your emotions and thoughts.

Walking away from an angry situation doesn't mean suppressing your feelings. Instead, it is a way to better understand your feelings so that when you express yourself, you do not give power to the anger or to another person.

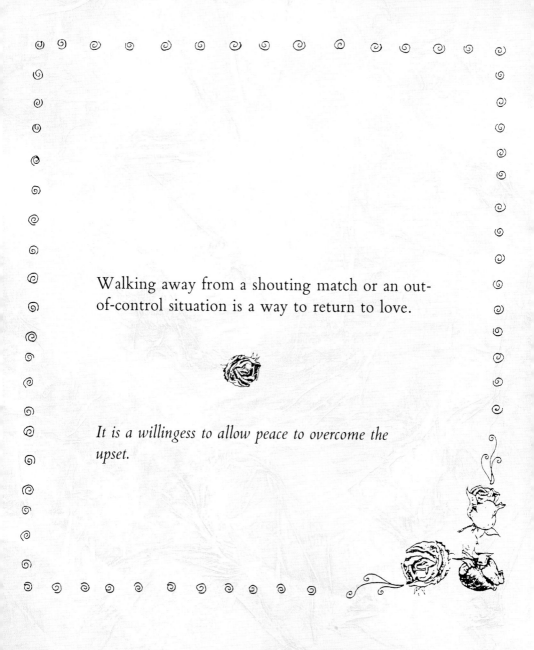

Walking away from a shouting match or an out-of-control situation is a way to return to love.

It is a willingess to allow peace to overcome the upset.

E X pect the Best

Everything present in our lives, at this moment, is a product of our belief system. Look around and see what you have allowed yourself to receive.

If you want outside conditions to improve, change your inner thoughts. The results will follow. It *is* that simple.

Whatever the conscious mind thinks and believes, the subconcious mind identically creates, so set your goals high.

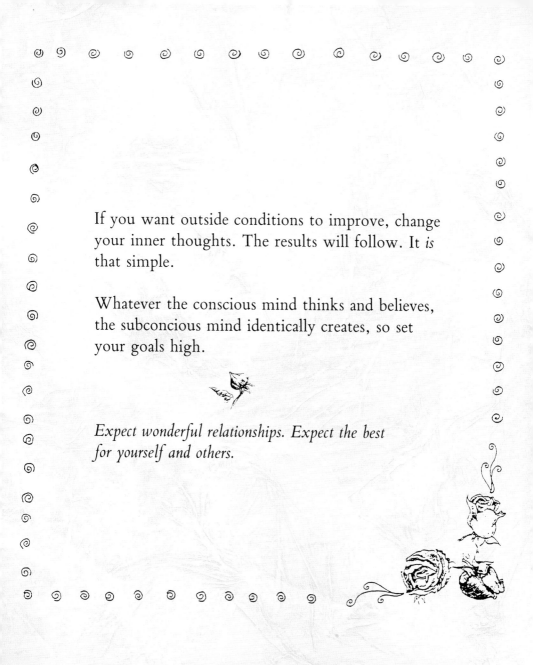

Expect wonderful relationships. Expect the best for yourself and others.

Say *Yes!*

Yes is a very empowering word. It signifies agreement, confirmation, and permission to move forward with your ideas.

Make room for more Yes's in your life. Let go of the no's that are holding you back (no money, no time, no love, etc.).

Say "Yes!" to change. Let love flow through your mind, body, and affairs.

Notice how much happier you feel when you say "Yes!" to life. Your heart bursts with joy.

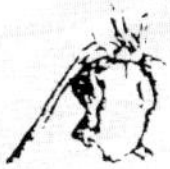

Accept the gift of an abundant life.

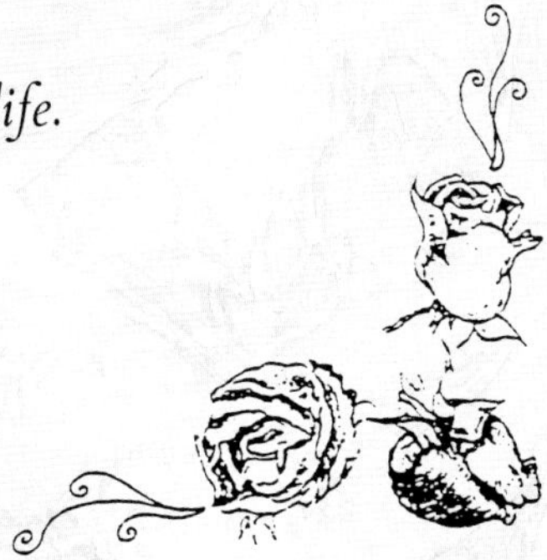

"Zero-In" on the Good in Others

Each of us is a divine spirit living in a human body. Look to the spirit of each person you come into contact with for a true connection. Zero-in on the divinity of that person.

You will feel an exchange of love taking place when you see people as they really are. Love is accepting and kind, never jealous or mean. It rejoices in the beauty of another.

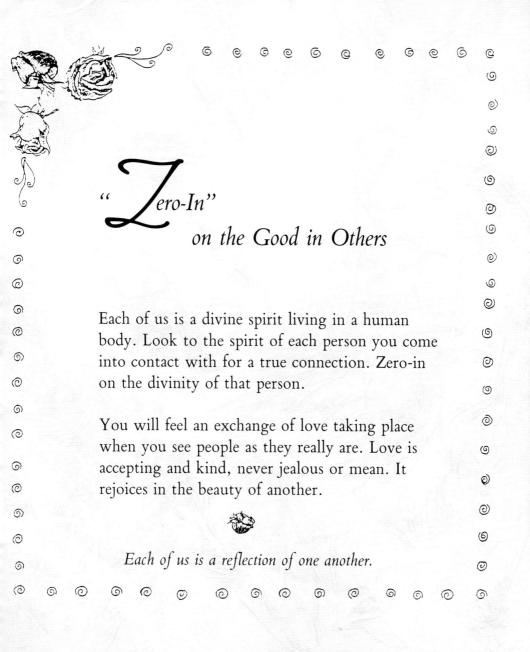

Each of us is a reflection of one another.

Suzanne Hirabayashi
is a graduate of the USC School of Journalism
and is also the author of the children's book
Under the Orchard Tree. She has been on a
spiritual journey since childhood and attends
the Agape Church of Religious Science
in Santa Monica, California. She lives
with her husband, Keith,
and their son, Jake.

We hope you have enjoyed
this book and invite you to consider
reading other books from DeVorss Publications
by calling 800.843.5743 for a free copy of our catalog.
We will gladly send the information you need
to help you along your spiritual journey.

Thank You.